THE UNEXPLAINED

ATLANTIS

BY TROY MICHELS

BELLWETHER MEDIA · MINNEAPOLIS, MN

Are you ready to take it to the extreme?
Torque books thrust you into the action-packed world
of sports, vehicles, mystery, and adventure. These books
may include dirt, smoke, fire, and dangerous stunts.
WARNING: read at your own risk.

Library of Congress Cataloging-in-Publication Data

Michels, Troy.
 Atlantis / by Troy Michels.
     p. cm. -- (Torque: The unexplained)
 Summary: "Engaging images accompany information about Atlantis. The combination of
high-interest subject matter and light text is intended for students in grades 3 through 7"--
Provided by publisher.
 "Torque."
 Includes bibliographical references and index.
 ISBN 978-1-60014-585-8 (hardcover : alk. paper)
 1. Atlantis (Legendary place)--Juvenile literature. I. Title.
 GN751.M53 2011
 001.94--dc22   2010034778

This edition first published in 2011 by Bellwether Media, Inc.

Printed in the United States of America, North Mankato, MN.

010111 1176

CONTENTS

CHAPTER 1
A CIVILIZATION VANISHES........ 4

CHAPTER 2
WHAT WAS ATLANTIS?........10

CHAPTER 3
SEARCHING FOR ANSWERS..... 16

GLOSSARY 22

TO LEARN MORE................ 23

INDEX................................24

A CIVILIZATION VANISHES

Atlantic Ocean

?
?
?
?

Mediterranean Sea

According to **ancient** legend, Atlantis was a large island at the center of a great **civilization**. Most people believe it was located in the Atlantic Ocean or the Mediterranean Sea.

Legend holds that Atlantis
tried to attack the Greek city
of Athens around 9600 B.C.
When the attack failed, disaster
struck. Earthquakes shook Atlantis.
Giant waves rose up around the
island. The civilization crumbled in
a single day and night. Atlantis has
never been seen again.

In 360 B.C., the Greek writer Plato wrote about Atlantis. He claimed that the story of Atlantis had been passed down for thousands of years. However, many people believe that he made the story up. No one has found proof that Atlantis ever existed.

Plato

SUNKEN STATUES

Plato wrote that Atlantis had many great works of art. Among them was a large statue of Poseidon, the Greek god of the sea.

CHAPTER 2
WHAT WAS ATLANTIS?

Strait of Gibraltar →

Mediterranean Sea

Atlantic Ocean

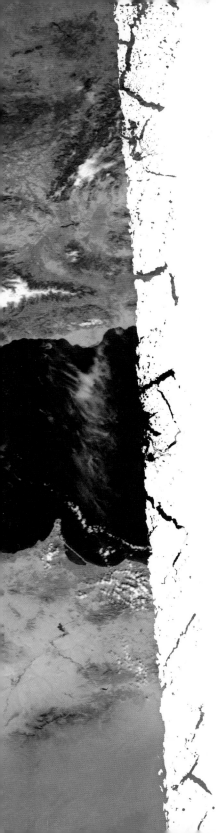

Plato describes Atlantis as an ancient power of both land and sea. The civilization may have thrived for thousands of years before it vanished.

The size and location of Atlantis remain mysteries. Some people think it was just an island city. Others think it was an entire **continent**. Plato wrote that it sat in front of the **Pillars of Hercules**. This is a landmark in the **Strait of Gibraltar**. The strait connects the Atlantic Ocean to the Mediterranean Sea.

An Indian legend tells of a sunken land off the coast of India called Kumari Kandam. Some people believe that Atlantis and Kumari Kandam are the same island!

KUMARI KANDAM

Many **theories** about Atlantis describe it as a unique civilization. Some people believe that it had advanced technology for its age. Others think the people of Atlantis had magical powers. People have even wondered if **aliens** helped build Atlantis.

Possible Locations of Atlantis

Place

The Bermuda Triangle

Bimini

The Canary Islands

Crete

The Indian Ocean

Malta

Sicily

Spartel Bank

Description

The Bermuda Triangle lies east of Florida. It is known for the many planes and ships that have disappeared there.

The remains of a road and sunken ruins lie under the Caribbean waters around Bimini.

The Canary Islands lie west of the Strait of Gibraltar in the Atlantic Ocean. Some people believe these islands are remnants of Atlantis.

Crete is an island in the Mediterranean Sea. A huge tsunami hit the island around 1500 B.C. and wiped out the Minoan civilization.

Indian legend describes a land called Kumari Kandam that sank beneath the waves of the Indian Ocean.

Malta is an island in the Mediterranean Sea near Greece. It was home to several ancient civilizations.

A temple on the Mediterranean island of Sicily matches some descriptions of temples on Atlantis.

Spartel Bank may have stood above sea level thousands of years ago, but the rising sea level submerged it. It lies near the Strait of Gibraltar.

CHAPTER 3
SEARCHING FOR ANSWERS

Many people believe that the legend of Atlantis is true. They continue to search for possible locations of its ruins. Others think the story of Atlantis is nothing more than a **myth** that has survived for thousands of years.

Those who believe that Atlantis existed have many theories about how it sank into the ocean. One theory is that the sea level rose and covered the island. **Skeptics** say this would have taken more than one day and night to happen.

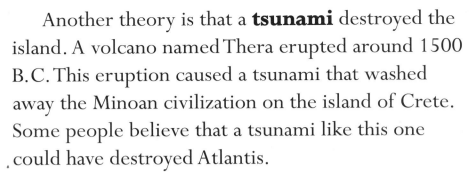

Another theory is that a **tsunami** destroyed the island. A volcano named Thera erupted around 1500 B.C. This eruption caused a tsunami that washed away the Minoan civilization on the island of Crete. Some people believe that a tsunami like this one could have destroyed Atlantis.

A MIGHTY ERUPTION

Thera's eruption may have been similar
to the eruption of Krakatoa in 1883. Krakatoa
created a tsunami about 120 feet (37 meters)
high in the waters around Indonesia.

sonar

People continue to search for Atlantis. Many use **sonar** to look for ruins on the ocean floor. They examine **satellite** photos for clues of a civilization beneath the sea. Do you think they will ever find anything? Or will Atlantis remain nothing more than a legend?

GLOSSARY

aliens—beings from another planet

ancient—occurring thousands of years ago

civilization—a developed, advanced society

continent—a very large land mass

myth—a story passed down from generation to generation for hundreds of years; most people believe myths are not true.

Pillars of Hercules—rock formations that mark one end of the Strait of Gibraltar

satellite—an object placed into orbit high above Earth, usually for communication purposes

skeptics—people who do not believe in something

sonar—machinery that uses sound waves to detect objects underwater

Strait of Gibraltar—a narrow waterway that connects the Atlantic Ocean to the Mediterranean Sea

theories—ideas that try to explain why something exists or happens

tsunami—an enormous wave, often caused by an earthquake or a volcanic eruption

TO LEARN MORE

AT THE LIBRARY

DeMolay, Jack. *Atlantis: The Mystery of the Lost City.* New York, N.Y.: PowerKids Press, 2007.

Hamilton, Sue. *Lost Cities.* Edina, Minn.: ABDO Pub. Co., 2008.

Martin, Michael. *Atlantis.* Mankato, Minn.: Capstone Press, 2007.

ON THE WEB

Learning more about Atlantis is as easy as 1, 2, 3.

1. Go to www.factsurfer.com.

2. Enter "Atlantis" into the search box.

3. Click the "Surf" button and you will see a list of related Web sites.

With factsurfer.com, finding more information is just a click away.

INDEX

9600 B.C., 6
1500 B.C., 18
360 B.C., 8
aliens, 12
art, 9
Athens, 6
Atlantic Ocean, 4, 5, 10, 11
civilization, 5, 6, 11, 12, 18, 20
continent, 11
Crete, 18
earthquakes, 6
India, 12
Indonesia, 19
Krakatoa, 19
Kumari Kandam, 12
legend, 5, 6, 12, 17, 20
location, 11
magical powers, 12

Mediterranean Sea, 5, 10, 11
myth, 17
Pillars of Hercules, 11
Plato, 8, 9, 11
Poseidon, 9
proof, 8
ruins, 17, 20
satellite, 20
sea level, 17
size, 11
skeptics, 17
sonar, 20
Strait of Gibraltar, 10, 11
technology, 12
theories, 12, 17, 18
Thera, 18, 19
tsunami, 18, 19
volcano, 18

The images in this book are reproduced through the courtesy of: Jon Eppard, front cover, pp. 12-13, 16-17; Alfonso de Tomas, pp. 4-5; Juan Martinez, pp. 6-7, 20-21; The Art Archive/Alamy, p. 8; Racheal Grazias, p. 9; NASA Images, pp. 10-11, 11 (small); Shannon Stent, p. 18; Martin Van Lokven/Foto Natura/ Getty Images, p. 19; NOAA/Science Photo Library, p. 20 (small)